PENNING
PAPER MOTHS

POETRY

BY
TRISHA LEIGH SHUFELT

PENNING
PAPER MOTHS

POETRY

BY
TRISHA LEIGH SHUFELT

"Moths are nocturnal poets of the invisible,
weaving dreams in the dark."
Author unknown

For Candice

CONTENTS

7

Judge a moth by the beauty of its candle.

Rumi

The Still Grey of Mourning

Between then and now,
the still grey of mourning
delays Day's awakening
mystery veils Autumn's Fire
pales pallet to lost potential

from isolating windows, eyes nictate,
naked limbs curl in retreating fetal dream
dewy chill, moths Memory
then disappears in silent death

neith the burgeoning brume
lake Loons break grieving quietus
echoing daily struggle
as bed sheets unfurl
like amber chanterelles
greeting another day without you.

Inanimate

I am the silent stone
edges rubbed smooth
by endless walks, witness
to a thousand worries
marinated in sweat
and fabled dreams

I am sleep and spin
revelation and rancor
I am shaped shadow
finger mothed madness
stained by kissing wishes
and salted sorrow

I am more of you
than riverbed
from which you took
more secrets than soil
more spirit than mineral

I am more than
the timeless seasons
spent waiting for a purpose.

The Story of the Wild Hunt

Evening's dampness
drowned better judgment
I stood upon a knife's edge
consumed in Mercurial's moment
walk me to my car

your expression could not veil thought
reading me like a poem
hidden inside the sweetness
of the darkest plum

back-alley shadows
blended us black
arresting senses
competing with deafening silence
and 2 a.m.'s last call
thrumming my ears

behind my eyes
a salt damn broke
our parted lips raked raw
failed to protest
inescapable surrender
as passing headlights lit us
like fireflies awakening the dark
with dreaming color.

Moledro

Your tongue is a feather
painting poetry
on the ceiling of my Soul
your breath, a hymn
from the Book of Life—
birds escaping an open cage
wing tipped in sacred ink

I've always known you
enchanted forest
reaving my peace
brooding neith my skin
heating flesh, sanguine
I'm drunk
on your holy wine
I lust for the art
your madness brings

I seek shelter
in unspoken prayers—
choke on confessions
my lips cannot reveal
I run around rosaries
biting back hidden hope
longing for absolution
in the church of your eyes.

Morpheus

I dream of woodland whispers
brushy willow tree sighs
Autumn mysteries
alighting the eyes
in virescent amber revers

I long for lanceolate leaves
trysts daring to tease
bare skin secrets
neith hidden lacy veil
awakening velvet trail
blushed in desire's sweetness—

I yield to Love's succulent fruit
feast with unbridled weakness
splendor in hushing softness
of nature vining nakedness
after trembling ground and root

days turn to dusky wonder
ignite moonlit moths to wander
pendulous cascades turn glaucous
Morpheus dreams blissful quietus
where echoes remain ubiquitous—
kissing pleasure's wing
in diaphanous distant thunder.

Between the Lines

Poet to my soul
roves golden gorse
in his garden of words
proffers sweet scented balm
for ink to soothe
scar's sharp envelope

his face veins every leaf
absorbs Autumn's fire
bleeds sunlit colors
honey, gold, and umber
from his Taurean eyes

yet, he is a bird
blown from Heaven's breath
angels feather his skin
silver sinews his wings
with hymns bramble born
in redemption's razor

poetry vines all seasons
within his secret garden
nestle me neith fingered soil
feed me sweet apple heartbeats
thundering the ground
where love is fire
kissing the bloom.

Bee Stings

You are born
of the honeyed hive
kissed by the bee
who feeds hungry souls
on plump poetry apples
cast in twilight gold

you are born
of the embracing day
loved by stars
dreaming of wind
swaying sleepy willow
fingers over green lovers
drunk on celestial dew

you are a book
of sacred mysteries
marrying mouths
in silent oneness—
an antidote mortals covet
hidden within
the sweet sting of your ink.

Pollen

Need—
as natural as breath
floats our essence
mouth to mouth
breath for life

Soul food
pollen for the bee
insect to sweetness
moth to flame
ivy vining our veins

lost within your lore
a portent to my core
seeking no rescue
from the drowning
draw of we.

Sunday Service

Spiral dance
desperation's kiss
ripe, sweet cherries
staining lips
skin's musky mist
salts tangled tryst
sweat-soaked sheets—
affections after bliss

empty coffee cups
cigarettes hiss
weave away hours
unawareness
smoke hazes
dreaming abyss
our limbs like trees
inosculating oneness.

Unpacking Peace

Peace is sinking into hues of blue
slow glow luminescence
twilight fireflies amidst cricket song
sweet silencing defenses
moth shadows neith summer moon
ripe apple, honeysuckle to taste
tremolo of speckled lake loons
morning skin's tangled embrace
poetry by ambient fireside
well-smoked, pear wood churchwarden
memory sighs as we, two, confide
secrets of day-dying burdens.

Night and Day

Shadows dovetail light
creaming galaxies collide
inside coffee cups—
yours handmade
mine, store-bought, cracked
fading flowers, like memories

silence sits between steam
trees watch us
through open windows
exhaling leaves
I ink into colored poetry

drinks imbibe time
betwixt questions and rhymes
winter winks pink insistence
flirts with gloaming sky
in the distance
crows gather
night's rowdy roost

our cups sit quiet, washed
awaiting another day.

Lace Curtains

We were succulents seeking sun
the world spinning
days of *never enough*
my inner thighs, a canvas of
pearlized art for sticky fingers
living off candy and naked need
swollen and rosy with ache

we were antidotes and addiction
promising to quit
when we'd tired of
sex, coffee, and Keats.

Skyclad

Wrap me
in skyclad skin
restless with night
let me be the salted sea
unfiltered and untamed
you, lucid, lithe
in cerulean dreams
let us crash currents
into unexplored abyss
in mystery's depths,
we are infinite
inking life's breath
in spiral's dance
we are reborn
graced in lunar pull
untamed by rational reason
we root and rise
biological in need
we inosculate as trees do
fed on the soil of self
we nurture our nature
memories made in our eyes
discover what is lost
reflect what is needed
mirror who we are
hidden within each other.

Kissing the Wild

Sweet cadence
escapes rose petal lips
teeming with sigh

desire's longing
flavors your tongue—
a thousand endless summers
damp in wild dreaming
become quenched in expectation

I would starve on loud hope
if only to feast on whispers
blossoming from your mouth.

Penning Paper Moths

Paper moths live
off the salt of your neck,
breed butterfly hope
in the flower,
become heavenly bower
where chrysalis wings
unfold stained glass hymns
on ivory keys still holding
a breathless note

turns into a ceaseless siren, afloat
in an unabashed naked dream,
and bathes in Spring's morning dew
until she is the ink you drink,
and sapphire skies you eye
before silence snakes your sleep

to love you in metaphors
steeped in shadow's sorrow,
whispering widowed wants
back into being—
the hiraeth you seek
is the ghost
who haunts your poetry.

Poet Gone Mad

He found me
in a house of remembrance
one created in childhood illusion
steeped in storms succeeding delusion
and embers of everlasting hope
he'd long surrendered to myth

He spoke to me
in captured thoughts
where eyes meet, silence hushes
air thickens with fingertip brushes
rushing pale skin with the need
one aches to appease with a kiss

He loved me
like a poet gone mad
one whose Soul left its center
as though I were a muse without measure
and every pleasure was a metaphor
Time endeavored to reave from his pen

He left me
fragmented and in between
as remnants of his retreating dream
clinging to Memory's mournful ephemeral
like sky grasps colors, temporal
dissolving into inevitable dusk.

I'll fly through the candle's mouth like a singeless moth.

Sylvia Plath

Harvest Time

Remains of day
well salted eyes
stormy seas spume
shadowed cries

ancient song
rake shores
reap secrets
held too long

unlace thoughts
haunting fragile peace
torture metaphors
time endeavors to lease

thoughts swirl
like autumn leaves
crashing ground
in colorful sheaves—

harvest time
for regrets and thieves.

Green Girl

Ophelia's thoughts stew
day's remains fill with rue
amidst breathless storms
worms eat pansy wilt

battered and broken
libertine warnings forsaken
feminine fardels are born
nothing to barter, lend, or be

Ophelia's haunted eyes
reflect tumbled good-byes
promises he made to wed—
pray, love, remember?

every tendered flower
vining her heavenly bower
like her Master, her father,
Green Girl made a good end

sweets to her sweetheart
pearl to his embattled heart
chaste treasures discarded,
worthless, ungelded

Hamlet shattered with a sigh
black stars fell from his eyes

buried truth, doubt, and lies
in love's steep, thorny dark
wreckage awaits the poetic.

Colors

She is Autumn's wilt
shadow chasing
remaining light
farther from
wild red hope
further toward
winter's white

still, she senses
an underlying note
pink-petaled sweetness
perfumes and floats

distant memories
sluice to blue
tangle in threads
of youth's rearview

now barren to blossoms
she foxtails brown
gasps for breaths
fearful to drown

neith the hollow
of a pale full moon
competing with darkness
looming too soon

white moths mottle
longing to rest
curl wings inward
protecting what's left

still, she waits to see
what colors come
to court her door.

Forever Between

roots and sky
tumbled bees
and poet's cries

trees that grieve
their colored thoughts
spaces and places
time forgot

discovering secrets
neith a skirt
navigating trust
despite the hurt

unearthing shadows
disguised as truth
unfolding dreams
chasing pursuits

navigating life
betwixt and between
wanting to hide
longing to be seen.

Heavy Pockets

Leafy boats float
down the river
colors twinkling
like Christmas lights

laden with distraction
I cast a pocket stone
rubbed smooth by time
into her widening mouth

she accepts
releases in response
rippling surface
breaking apart serenity

malcontent, the boats
scatter, others circle
one appears to sink, yet
reemerges to join the flotilla

like the leafy bobber, dank earth
infused with wet wool,
rises to my nose
I am breathing again

raw but numb
I replace my castaway

with an acorn, press its tip
between finger and thumb

flesh bleeds with life
copper, dirt, and salt
meet curious tongue
I wonder if the river *feels*

does it feel like me

twilight approaches
stretches longs shadows
her weary travelers
in need of rest

I'm weary too

distant Mistle Thrush song
competes with the current
voices rewinding, repeating
sorrow too much to bear

the river is an open pocket
poetry and lyrics, forever flowing
hours upon hours of liquid thoughts
home my pockets

I feel heavy

The Season for Dying

The *Season for Dying* debuts
against an arid Winter sky
exhaling smoldering embers
in solemn Angel's goodbye

her once shiny, golden apples
bake and blacken burnished ground
sparkle wind with ashen sequins
like starlets' discarded gowns

what remains in her lost colors
when reality paints disbelief—
a monochrome human cinema
of memories buried beneath

faces peer through broken windows
beacons of hope in endless night
no small actors nor parts to play
all cast and equal roles, despite

dark debris of scattered tender
amongst the Precambrian stones
knows the sorrow they surrender
in trusting Tomorrow's unknowns.

The Poet Must Die

I am a curiosity made tremulous
by tomorrow's retreat
no longer seeking moonlight
I am light itself, trapped
in present predicament
still with life, I flutter

inside a four-square frame
edging contemplation's ledge
thoughts corner the mind
behind the pain, I am the moth
inside the pane, I'm dying

life seeks no exit
yet fears transformation—
paper lantern wings
are stained-glass windows—
holy colors swallowing shadows
in Death's silent surrender

desperate for life
become forgotten flowers
drying in a glass vase,
muted, preserved

without pinning canvas
perception falls away for perspective

I see myself for the first time, free
in my reflection, I am
a monumental consequence, I am
a revelation encapsulated
in a simple observation.

Inspired by the Death of the Moth
By Virginia Woolf 1942

Loss

The wind winnows
letters writ upon leaves
mourning dew
coats my face

there is no solace
no gentle sleep
quiets your loud absence
or weathers the wilt

I shadow your invisible bedside
playwright unsaid words
and patron your scent
still ghosting downy pillows

I am captive to clock strike
unpinning memories
like silent moths
that hinter the brain.

All Aboard

I am a train
my skin, a punched ticket
my veins, a track
moving me
through life

as I breathe
my heart churns
a chugging engine
huffing uphill
careening down
glimpsing passing moments

I board wandering travelers
some stowaway
hiding their intentions
in couchette compartments
others depart without notice—

inevitable stations
known and unknown
whistle warnings in my ears
reducing inviolate space
rending perspective lost.

Cheap

I'm afraid I'm a fraud
dross sours my skin
like perfume I can't afford

words jumble—
an incoherent mass
of rambles clog pipes
in need of snaking

I stare at blank paper
ghosting my thoughts
nothing muses my malady
or cures curdling complacencies

I've managed to manipulate
years of shrink-wrapped fallacies
polluting my inner pulpit

where are the long shadows
I've come to call friends

even their familiar blackness
fails me now
as though, they too, fear
the light they long to be.

The Art of Deceit

Sleepless hours await the poem
born of thorny unforgiveness
silences without apology
sinks sighs inked on hollowed lines

bleeding unholy scripture
hope taints and colors rust truth
like bruised fruit entices
sweet center to rot

still, I'd swallow, willingly
eulogize endless questions
cloying with unanswered need

better to ingest homemade poison
than watch Time wreck and spoil
space between, with festering lies.

A Sprig of Thyme

I gave you a sprig
fresh from the vine
I left my garden's peace to you
tender flavors bittered in time
and grew a willow tree

pink, blue, and violet-hued, truth
colored thoughts of you
beware they said
neith roses red are thorns,
you may not see

for wide is the sun
seasoning the shoot, still, too,
breaks branch from fair tree,
and splits fruit, ripe with rot
to rue the pit within thee.

Inspired by the folk ballad A Sprig of Thyme and
Let No Man Steal Your Thyme variant written in 1689.

Into the Leaves

We let the wind
pick apart our presence
untied wings
disguised as pretense and
let them fall to the forest floor—
offerings to the copper gods
whose sweet-scented poetry
pressed leaves
tinged with Autumn blush
into skin's awakening book.

The Players

Can we sit together
no space between
watch our sepia cinema
share overpriced concessions
we can no longer afford

we chose this reel
leached from loss
gave ourselves over
to grieving lines
salted sorrow's lens
with and without sound

neither Star nor Director
but Producers writing scripts
bleeding words never read...
too drunk on dark comedy
an irony neither could sober
nor find funny
despite punchline

the players you see
were never black and white
they low hum electric color
hidden behind shades of grey.

Blind Window

I cannot unfold, unpack,
hush screaming ears,
or blind visions on repeat

I cannot untangle nerves
near the surface while
others silently root their ill

there is no remedy
I can pour down my throat
no distraction I can court

words fail to feed
the burgeoning hole
there is no forgiveness without a lie

there is only malady manifesting memory
bleeding into the barren loss of you.

Little Red

I lie in stinging nettle
bleeding glass ruin
I wonder,
is it safe to whisper
what pricks my pain

she, who lives for fairytales
should be warned—
dark alchemy brews
beneath Sylvan's shadowy soil

it's breeding time for
insatiable, desperate serpents
despite glutted apple bellies
she is ripe for their picking

they, who kiss with hissing sweetness
love her temptation before the fall
they, who court with clenching prowess
whose musky wool faces enthrall

assault her senses with skillful silkiness
binding bones with beguiling ease
carve maker's marks until acceptance
in the end, what's left, time will reave

do not cheat me

the awe behind your silence—
your masked judgment
we've all been there
wrecked vessels set adrift

endless Lacrimosa
salting horizons—
hoping hymns fill
unquenchable need for love
or guide moths seeking
a lighthouse in their eyes

it's not a simple thing
to pretend anguish is a halcyon—
an antidote to heavy truth
pushing aside what occupies
the rooms of the mind

aren't those the same things
that scar the heart
or allow one to feel
at peace with pain
when trust we've known
becomes tainted refrain.

The Visitor

You wreck the night's peace
tiny bird
pecking my stained-glass gaze

I say
I am a poet bleeding
truth's ambiguous ink
from sorrow's salted wound

you stop
cock your head, listen—
start again as tapping pen
a ticking clock

a match
igniting smoke remembrance
disguised as best intention
burns every quiet corner

hidden guilt
and cloying desperation
over shadows dying magnolia scent
still clinging to white crumpled paper

flowers ascending the floor like
death moths eating unsaid words—
I'm sorry
I'm sorry

I'm sorry.

Fallen Fruit

We carry baskets of bruises
around a universal tree
counting our sins and losses
lamenting another three

allow the rest to drop and rot
to grieve amongst the leaves
let the earth do her bidding
where darkness favors release

all questions have answers
only time discloses the *why*—
revelations birthed from chaos
echo meaning in goodbye.

Lovely in dye and fan,
A-tremble in shimmering grace,
A moth from her winter swoon
Uplifts her face

Walter de la Mare

The Echo of Old Books

Pressed memories
purl pages,
mute flowers,
sepia stain photographs,
threaded with silver hair

poetry's ageless ink
breathing lines
birth, love, life
death

only Time would reave life
of its colors,
yet preserve its beauty
for another's hands
within onion skin pages
of beloved past.

Night Garden

Window reflections grieve rain
snail time's restless need
tangle thoughts
flutter wordless moths
in my throat

I seek us
neith haunted moon luminescence
in hidden seeds ruminating
paper flower poetry rhymes
awaiting bloom
an inked labyrinth
lost in longing

Are you there
in brambled embrace
scar mapping flesh petals
shadow weaving roads
back to oneness or

will time brown
our bower blossoms
drown these purple lines
heavy with dew
spiral us into an inevitable soul frise

say no, and find me, love

lean me over tomorrow's ledge
blaze this sodden night
with your bright tender
love me again
like a metaphor gone mad.

Release Me

The day we met,
you netted my breath
moths filled my throat
their wings weighted
with honeyed words

I remained mute,
stuck, and vulnerable
the way Autumn's last leaf,
weak with drench,
clings to branch,
hesitating surrender's fall

even now, I fear
ferrying poetry rivers
written in your name
where dreamy depths draw
desperation like Naiad's song
to watery grave

still, I dive willingly
shatter like glass
against your salt
lay spent in rosy, blue colors—
a mosaic you sculpt
with your pen

my fallen angel of words
where do I draw the line
when you no longer read me
from left to right
when my skin is no longer
pleasing parchment to your pen

release me to muse and myth
before I become ink
you care not to sink
or stale, scratched words
in a discarded prose

release me
while I still breathe
perhaps then,
I will find words to thank you.

The Poetry of the Earth is Never Dead

Every poet who has
taken pen to paper
pressed back against oak
sought shade neith weeping willow

or gazed upon Heaven's blue, whilst
lying on lush green fairy moss
has surely left their tenet with time
upon nature's tapestry

I've walked in the twilight glow
of their long shadows, chasing light
I've held hands with their words
and pressed imagination to my lips

the poetry of the earth is never dead
when memories lift their veil
and from soil, seek the softest
Autumn leaf that harvests

the remainders of day
and remembrances of night—
in graceful descent, poets whisper,
we are still writing.

1ˢᵗ italicized line in stanza four from
On the Grasshopper and Cricket by John Keats, 1816

Dreams of Aquila

Storms gathered
in my breast
you held me
like a taut bowstring

fly me to Aquila
this world lacks color
we are losing light
I want to witness the stars
I want to be someone other than who I am

the night faded to blue
in the distance,
eyrie birds were singing
a plucked chord
interrupted me
overshadowing reality

I skirted it away—
a misplaced memory
fell into denial
cradled by fog and
retreating dream's
morning thaw.

Embroidered Mist

Eternity's needle weaves you
against Autumn feathered sky
I see you through a mist—
of form and colors vitrified

spectral shadows dance
neith lacy linen dress—
moonlit goddess enchantments
born of Starlight noblesse

your rosy ribbons vein and wave
in tangled hemlock, raven nest
where death knots a fairy briar
of somber secrets and thorny unrest

pricking fingers are sticky plums
honey thick with crimson wine—
I'll fashion you a Hellebore crown
dripping sweet delirium from your mind

my fragile beauty, my moth in a jar
where youth grows pale, and spectre-thin
I long to *leave the world unseen,*
and with thee fade away into the forest dim

Alas, light breaks stained-glass windows
she retreats into nightingale song

and is no more than a dream devoured
in this sleeper's unforgiving dawn.

Italicized lines from John Keats' letter to
Fanny Brawne and Ode to a Nightengale 1819

Dolce Far Niente

When your mind is muddied
thick with a thousand thoughts
when fear overshadows fortitude
clouds your shoulds with should nots

take a languid moment
exhale caged tenacious breath
ease endless squeaky wheels
turn off false light's demanding net

let pause bring you inner peace
invite silence into your space
spread it wide like a comfy quilt
let nothing speed your pace

nestle neith its childlike fort
listen to Memory's lost lilt
stories of fierce dragons
fantasy worlds imagination built

sail pirate ships into tranquility
measure time by moon or sun
speak to stars quietly
there's nothing to rush or get done

be the hopeful *ingenue*
one who believes in dreams

she is in the wings, waiting
when life falls apart at the seams

trust, you are protected
underneath flowerbed threads
the wind whispers, *dolce far niente*
rest easy, there is nothing to dread.

Dolce far niente-Italian for sweetness of doing nothing.

Aging Grace

Time covets
wraps choking vine
around harvested branches

you are hanging on
last Autumn fruit
rimed in pernicious frost
fearful to fall

upon unforgiving path
brede in madness
or childlike wonder

you tumble backward
into delusion's illusions
drest in pointillist dots

with you,
I'll view this world
from windowless rooms
I'll bear piercing nettles
pricking your peace
I'll court bees
brooding your brain

I'll anchor you
far from Time's picking reach

I'll press pieces of myself
into your sleeping book
I'll crown your head
with twining flowers,
where fruit, remains sweet
upon Memory's bower

you will remain,
evermore, bright star
amongst dimming night
you will remain my Spring
in your seasons of dying light.

Inspired by Bright Star & To Autumn by John Keats

Muse

I am moth wing whispers illuminating **an**
unborn thought—an epiphany igniting an **hour**
of soul desperation—beckoning you **near**
like bees to the blossom. I am the rose to **your**
ink and honeyed muse to your **mouth**
only a poet understands. I am bramble **and**
bone, prickling your skin with knowing need. **I'd**
seize a thousand storms as stories for you to **spin**
and wrest the sea of its salt to infuse **your**
blood with its haunting hue. There is no **breath**
I would not silence to speak **through**
your lips. I am the Autumn leaf, lush in longing for **a**
moment's breeze to fall into your dreaming **myth**.

Golden Shovel Poem inspired by Samuel Hurley's poem
Time's Lonely Attic from An Anthem for the Dreaming Lost.

Spells

Behind cracked corners
she's conjuring
stars out of sticks
spinning webs
into inked lines
siphoning spells
clenched between
pebble and rock

Within her reach
moths swarm dying light
draw ever-present shadows
into wing-singed truth—
poetry, she ignites
neith the lonely moon

Ashes for absolution
stones for strength
cut this grieving awareness
from bone's embrace

Once upon a time,
before the fall,
everyone was a virgin,
before doubt littered thoughts,
and spoiled myth with their ink.

A Reminder

If this is the end
if the world is riven to ruin
may we keep our memories
collected like Autumn leaves

each one, a colorful reminder
we found strength in fragility
grace in quiet hope
beauty amidst the chaos
peace in Season's surrender

deeper still,
may we remember simple things
a smile
a kindness
a kiss
a touch

how we forgave and forgot
trusted and feared not
imagined and dreamed
and all the wonders in between
becoming and letting go.

Soundless Sanctuary

Honor pain
in winter's exhale
weep saturnine offerings
upon the altar of night
under a pale paper moon

close your eyes and
surrender bereaved burdens
to its soundless sanctuary
until grief's release
eases deleterious dreams

there is peace in the stillness
of Nature's healing heart.

Advice from the Wind

Autumn spices the ground
curry, cayenne, and cardamon round
childhood thoughts beneath the foot—
rust in a dry book, saying

read me again

unfold the past that names you
cast away sorrows that claim you
lie down, rest, and root
neith majesty of Autumn's fruit

feed soil's withered weeds
comfort loon in the hidden reeds
paint petals picked too soon
ignite stars and birth dear moon

make a crown of fallen leaves
drink honey kissed by golden bees
fashion brushes from blades of grass
swirl the sky with clouds that pass

sail each sunset into the sea
let its colors sweeten your tea
live life without rhyme or reason
love your life and all its seasons

find ease in the breeze
and guidance in the trees
poetry in descending leaves
there is much to perceive

from hymns on the wind—
read me again
yesterday's lore opening doors
to peace, time forgot.

Eulogy to the Past

Age tarnishes
memory and object
yet beauty does not live
on the surface of precious things,
it resides in determined decay
weathering, flaking,
chipping away pretense
until perfection becomes transcendent—
a transparent, radiant portal
pursuing the past
where foxtails reveal golden relics
waxed poetically through time
and deep lines become undead eulogies
of unrelenting hope that we, too—
may be remembered
amidst our encumbering dust.

Awakening

Silence shells your shadows
behind caged teeth
bites back answers
not found in another's bones
can't you see you're the poet?
penning your path
observing life's liminal lessons
real and unreal, woven ethereal
palm lines intersecting leaf veins
born of Creation's colors
curtain closed by fear
eclipsed in Doubt's illusion
speckled starlight awakening
inside the ebony hollow of your eyes
cavernous lens expanding
unleashing Truth's well-spring
drenching the desolate night with dew
that begs to blaze a new light
and rake the ground with knowing dawn.

We Shall Meet Again

Among woodland woven bramble
sparse Spring evanesces to smoke
branches frost neith lilac mantle
red berries button Winter's coat

dreams drift to streams, Oceanus
silver petals kiss our goodbyes
haunting spaces, interfluous
land of ashes and paradise

beyond Realm's liminal slumber
beyond its fields of Asphodel
mourning fades to silent wonder
amidst sweet cherry amarelle

we cross into Elysia
shining bright as the stars above
release pain for panacea
embraced again by those we love.

Acknowledgements

To Candice Louisa Daquin-thank you for your unwavering friendship and stellar editing skills. You mean more to me than I can possibly express.

To April Coppini for the use of her BEAUTIFUL Luna moth artwork on the cover. I am truly grateful to you.

To Samuel Hurley-Thank you for allowing me to utilize your brilliant line in the Golden Shovel poem Muse. Moreso, thank you for being an inspiring light to me. I am grateful to know you as friend and fellow poet in my lifetime.

To Andy and Patrick-I love you with all that I am.

Trisha Leigh Shufelt is an award-winning poet, self-taught mixed media artist, and breast cancer survivor. Trisha's work leans toward confessional poetry with an emphasis on nature. She often draws upon her own experience with addiction, anxiety, and loss. She is the author of several poetry books, including *The Ghosts of Nevermore*, winner of a 2023 Saturday Visiter Award from the Edgar Allan Poe House and Museum in Baltimore, MD. Her work has also appeared in several poetry anthologies.

Poetry Books by the Author

Liminal Lines- Poetry & Prose
Liminal Lessons- Poetry & Prose
Break & Bloom-Poetry & Prose
The Ghosts of Nevermore-Poetry, Prose & Short
Stories inspired by the works of Edgar Allan Poe- *2023*
Saturday Visiter Award Winner through the Poe House
& Museum of Baltimore, MD.
The Ghosts of Winterbourne-Poetry & Prose
Sunder the Silence-Poetry & Prose
Unearthing Nevermore-Golden Shovel Poetry
Inspired by Edgar Allan Poe
Avenoir Poetry & Prose

Poetry & Short Story Anthologies, Magazines, and online publications

Evermore 2 & 4-Raven's Quoth Press
300 South Street Publishing-
Love is Helpless
Immortal Tales
Shadow of the Soul
Quail Bell Magazine
Heretics, Lovers, and Madmen

Published under the pen Andaleigh Archer include-

The Underwood Wicked Fairytale Series
Underwood-A Wicked Beginning
Thorn Apple-A Wicked Spell
Quietus-A Wicked Ending
Maeve-A Wicked Beginning
The Promise ~A Faerie's Tale

Artist & Author works through Schiffer Publishing/RedFeatherMBS include-

The Poe Tarot- *Nominated for a 2022 Saturday Visiter Award through the Poe House & Museum of Baltimore, MD & winner of a Bronze 2022 COVR Visionary Award.*
The Everglow Divination System

Other works include-
Passion for Poetry-A poetry review journal for poets and poetry lovers

You can find out more about Trisha at www.trishaleighpoetry.com

"And I'll bury my soul in a scrapbook, with the photographs there and the moths."

Leonard Cohen